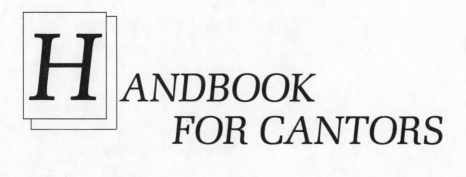

Handbook
FOR CANTORS

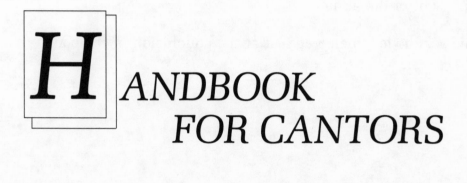

H ANDBOOK FOR CANTORS

Diana Kodner Sotak

Liturgy Training Publications

The author wishes to thank Michael Hay and Barry Moorhead for reading and offering advice on the manuscript. The appendix, ''An Evening of Recollection'' by Fred Moleck, originally appeared in the November/December 1987 issue of *Liturgy 80* and is reprinted with the consent of the author.

Music acknowledgments appear at the conclusion of the book.

Printed in the United States of America.

ISBN 0-930467-89-2

C ontents

Examples, Illustrations and Exercises

*I*ntroduction: The Cantor

The term "cantor" has several applications today. In Jewish worship it refers to the singer of holy songs who is a leader of prayer in a congregation. In Lutheran worship it is still sometimes used for the director of music in a congregation, a designation from the 17th century. The cantor in Roman Catholic worship is similar to these, and yet distinct.

As the church became institutionalized in its early centuries, so did various liturgical roles, including that of the cantor. The cantor was a member of the assembly who could chant psalms and alleluias. Such song was an important part of Christian liturgy. Later, choirs developed and took to themselves much of the singing that had belonged to the assembly and the cantor. The cantor disappeared, and song, which had been integral to the liturgy, eventually was heard only at the "high" Mass when the choir sang and the assembly listened.

The role of the cantor was restored to Roman Catholic liturgical practice by reforms of the Second Vatican Council. The liturgy envisioned by the Council demanded that the people assembled be full, conscious and active participants. Such a liturgy needs a cantor.

For some time after the Council, song leaders were used to encourage the participation of the assembly. Often this encouragement was no more than the announcing of page numbers and the singing of the people's parts into a microphone. Sometimes the song leader would attempt to "conduct" the assembly. Time has proven, however, that this kind of encouragement is very limited. While the visible participation of liturgical ministers in sung worship is encouraging to the assembly, it is the organ or other instruments which lead song. The amplification of a single voice over and above the singing of the assembly may actually be a deterrent to their full and active participation. Conducting the assembly is both superfluous and distracting.

The *General Instruction of the Roman Missal* is the principal post-conciliar description of the way we are to celebrate Mass. (It is printed at the front of the sacramentary, the book which contains the order of service and prayers for the Mass.) The *General Instruction* describes several ways that the cantor serves in the liturgy:

> There should be a cantor or choirmaster to direct and encourage the people in singing. If there is no choir, the cantor leads the various songs, and the people take their own part.   (#64)

> The chanter of the psalms is to sing the psalm or other biblical song between the readings. The cantor should be trained in the art of singing psalms and be able to speak clearly and distinctly.   (#67)

The role of cantor has come to signify a number of things. It is generally considered the ministry of the cantor to:

- lead moments of worship through solo song
- share in proclaiming the word of God, particularly as psalmist
- teach the assembly its songs, refrains and acclamations
- animate the sung worship of the assembly

The cantor is a member of the assembly who can and does serve the assembly in its worship. The cantor is never to be an outsider but one clearly identified with those gathered. The special charism of the cantor is to act as a catalyst for the sung expression of faith from within the assembly. While solo song is the cantor's primary vehicle for this, there are nonmusical ways in which a cantor must be able to communicate and to animate. Even the daily life of such a minister will affect that person's ability to serve as a leader of worship.

This ministry requires a great deal of competence. The cantor must be singer, proclaimer, liturgical minister and spiritual leader. The purpose of this book is to help cantors become proficient in their craft. The book is intended as a resource to which the cantor can return again and again. Not everything here is for the beginner; much will be challenging even to the experienced cantor. The book may be used by a group working together or by an individual. The person using the book alone should understand that it is often helpful to have the input of others when one is practicing an art that involves communication.

After this brief introduction, the book is organized into seven sections:

- the cantor's songs
- the cantor in liturgical celebration
- the eucharistic liturgy
- the cantor as a singer
- interpretation
- practice
- related concerns

These areas overlap and are interdependent, but they offer points of departure for discussion and study. Scattered throughout are practical recommendations, exercises and reference materials supporting the information provided. Many of these are set apart in boxes for easy reference. There is also an appendix offering a model for an evening of reflection for music ministers.

If cantors are to be effective in their ministry, they need a firm understanding of their role and its place in liturgical celebration. They need to understand their voices and so avoid and overcome flaws which detract from the expression of texts. They need to practice their ministry until it is fully a part of them and then to nurture what has been acquired. Such an approach will make this a joyful ministry for cantors and for those they serve.

How to Use This Book with a Group

When using this book with a group, the author recommends weekly sessions for a period of at least four weeks, more if possible. Begin with a reflective exercise such as the one suggested on page 21, and with some form of communal prayer (such as a simple form of evening prayer).

Allow time at each session for group discussion of previously assigned reading, gradually working through the book in this way and eventually incorporating additional reference materials. Some time should be spent on group vocal warm-up and on vocal exercises from the section on the cantor as a singer. The remainder of each session should be spent applying reading and vocalization to cantorial rendition. Each member of the group should have an opportunity to sing a psalm, litany or song. A leader and/or other group members should then offer constructive input.

The final session might be a gathering for an evening of reflection, using the model in the appendix. It is important for ministers to come together to pray and to reflect on what it means to serve.

Suggestions for Further Reading

Michael Connolly, *The Parish Cantor: Helping Catholics Pray in Song* (Old Hickory TN: Pastoral Arts Associates of North America, 1982). 46 pages.

James Hansen, *The Ministry of the Cantor* (Collegeville MN: The Liturgical Press, 1985). 40 pages.

Lawrence J. Johnson, *The Mystery of Faith: The Ministers of Music* (Washington DC: National Association of Pastoral Musicians, 1983). Pages 37-44.

The Cantor's Songs

The Psalms

The psalms constitute a large and significant body of material for which the cantor is responsible. They are integral to celebrating the liturgy of the hours, the eucharist, and most of the church's other rites. The psalms contribute in an essential way to the structure of these rites and to the content of our feasts and seasons.

The church's psalter includes the 150 psalms from the Book of Psalms. There are also a number of other poems, usually referred to as canticles, from both the Hebrew Scriptures and the New Testament. The New Testament itself tells how the psalter was prayed and cherished by Jesus and by those who followed him. The church continued to pray and sing these psalms and canticles finding in them a large and beautiful repertory. The psalms have taught us how to speak before God, alone and as a church. The psalms embrace all the passions and moods and conditions of humankind. Singing the psalms, our voices join with Jews and Christians of our day and of scores of generations.

In the eucharistic liturgy, the song between the readings is restricted to the psalter. The lectionary, the book that contains the order of scripture readings through the year, also designates the psalm for a given day or season of the liturgical year. The readings for Sundays are assigned on a three-year cycle. The specific year is indicated by [A], [B] or [C]. In the lectionary, the psalm designated for each day is placed between the first and second readings, but alternatives are also provided. These are the seasonal responses provided in the lectionary at #174, and the seasonal psalms at #175 which are intended for use on all the Sundays of a given season.

Look carefully at these seasonal psalms. Each of them—Psalm 96 at Christmastime or Psalm 51 during Lent, for example—constitutes a sort of theme song for its season, a source of meditation on the season that returns fresh and new each year. The seasonal psalms are particularly useful because of their ability to set a season apart. The repetition of one psalm over several weeks allows the assembly to know it by heart; only then are people truly able to make the psalm their own, to ponder its poetry and images and to learn this way of praying. And "this way of praying" is not simply one option among many but is the very model of all Jewish and Christian prayer.

Ways of Singing the Psalms with a Cantor

RESPONSORIAL

Although there are numerous ways of singing the psalms, the most common method is the responsorial form. This is the form designated for the psalm between the readings at Mass, but it is also used in celebrating the liturgy of the hours and at other rites such as penance services and the anointing of the sick. The name does not refer

---

Responsorial Psalms

Many fine musical collections of responsorial psalms are available, some of which are listed here:

ICEL Lectionary Music (GIA Publications, 7404 South Mason Avenue, Chicago IL 60638; 1982). Settings of some of the seasonal psalms and responses.

Joseph Gelineau, *The Gelineau Gradual* (GIA Publications, 1977). Settings of those portions of the psalter used for Sundays and principal feasts.

Psalms for the Cantor (World Library Publications, PO Box 2701, Schiller Park IL 60176; 1986). Settings of those portions of the psalter used for Sundays and feasts, as well as seasonal psalms, in seven volumes organized by liturgical season.

Respond and Acclaim (OCP Publications, PO Box 18030, Portland OR 97218-0030; 1987). Psalm refrains with corresponding tones for Sundays and feasts.

A good resource for psalmody within the liturgy of the hours is *Praise God in Song* (GIA Publications, 1979).

to making a "response" to a reading, but only to the form of rendition used. In this responsorial form the cantor or choir intones the refrain (often called the antiphon) which is repeated by the assembly. The cantor or choir continues with the singing of the first stanza (a stanza usually contains several verses of the psalm), and each stanza is followed by the return of the refrain, sung by the assembly. Such alternation continues until the psalm concludes with a final singing of the refrain.

The following is an example of the responsorial form.

Refrain:

Cantor: In the si-lent hours of night, bless the Lord.
All: In the si-lent hours of night, bless the Lord.

1. O come, bless the Lord, all you who serve the Lord,

who stand in the house of the Lord,

in the courts of the house of our God.

All: In the si-lent hours of night, bless the Lord.

2. Lift up your hands to the ho-ly place

and bless the Lord through the night.

All: In the si-lent hours of night, bless the Lord.

The following excerpt from the Canticle of the Lamb demonstrates a litany-like method of performing a psalm. This is a variation of the responsorial form. Notice the frequent return of the refrain.

In the responsorial method, the cantor's verses sometimes make use of a formula or "psalm tone." This is a simple melodic pattern in which a number of words are sung to a single pitch. The psalm verses may be "pointed" or otherwise marked to correspond to the specific tone. Traditional Gregorian psalm tones have been supplemented by many newly composed tones, such as those found in the *ICEL Lectionary Music* collection, *The People's Mass Book* choral edition (World Library Publications), *Respond and Acclaim* (Oregon Catholic Press) and *Worship* (GIA Publications).

The tones of the Gelineau psalms (named for the French composer Joseph Gelineau) exemplify another kind of formula, one based on rhythmic organization. *The Gelineau Gradual* offers complete instructions in the method of interpreting its psalms.

The following canticle is an example of a pointed text and its corresponding tone.

1. Let us give thanks to the Fàther
   for having made you wórthy
   to share the lot of the sáints in light.

2. He rescued us from the power of dàrkness
   and brought us into the kingdom of his beloved Són.
   Through him we hàve redemption,
   the forgiveness óf our sins.

3. He is the image of the invisible Gòd,
   the first-born of all créatures.
   In him everything in heaven and on earth wàs created,
   things visible ánd invisible.

4. All were created through hìm;
   all were created for hím.
   He is before all èlse that is.
   In him everything contínues in being.

5. It is he who is head of the body, the chùrch;
   he who is the begínning,
   the first-born òf the dead,
   so that primacy may be hís in everything.

Here is another method of marking a text for its corresponding tone. The intonation is a kind of introduction which occurs only at the beginning of a stanza. The tenor is a note to which a large portion of the psalm is chanted. The mediant provides melodic interest within the chanting of the psalm. It is usually denoted by an accent but here it is denoted by bold type (as is the final cadence).

O God, | you are my God whom I seek; '
    for you my flesh pines and my **soul** thirsts *
    like the earth, parched, lifeless and **with**out water.   *R.*

Thus have | I gazed toward you in the **sanc**tuary *
    to see your power **and** your glory,
For your kindness is a greater **good** than life; *
    my lips shall **glor**ify you.   *R.*

Thus will | I bless you **while** I live;*
    lifting up my hands, I will **call** upon your name.
As with the riches of a banquet shall my soul be **sat**isfied,*
    and with exultant lips my **mouth** shall praise you.   *R.*

Sometimes the "tone" has been written out with the text, as in the following excerpt.

Refrain

As morn - ing breaks I look to you, O God, to be my strength this day, al - le - lu - ia.

1. O God, you are my God, for you I long;
2. My body pines for you
3. So I gaze on you in the sanctuary
4. For your love is bet - ter than life,
5. So I will bless you all my life,
6. My soul shall be filled as with a banquet,
7. On my bed I remember you. On you I muse through the night
8. My soul clings to you;
9. Glory to the Father, and to the Son,
10. As it was in the be - ginning,

1. for you my soul is thirst - ing.
2. like a dry, weary land with - out wa - ter.
3. to see your strength and your glo - ry.
4. my lips will speak your praise.
5. in your name I will lift up my hands.
6. my mouth shall praise you with joy.
7. for you have been my help;/
    in the shadow of your wings I re - joice.
8. your right hand holds me fast.
9. and to the Ho - ly Spir - it.
10. is now and will be for ev - er. A - men.

This is an example of Gelineau psalmody.

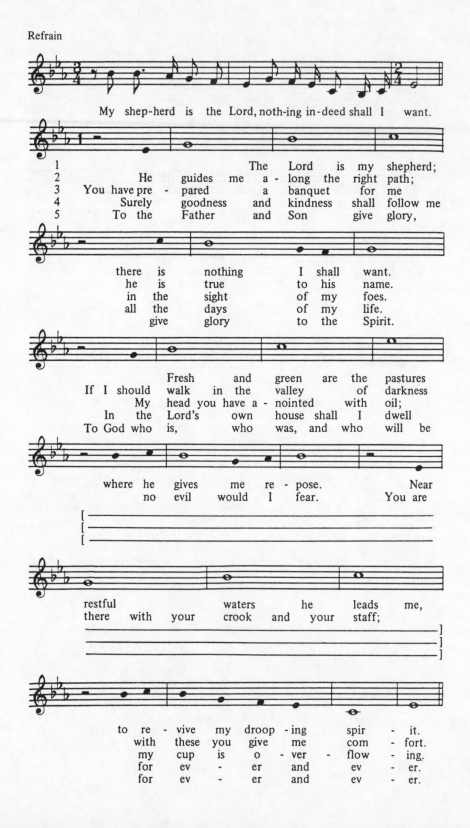

Refrain

My shep-herd is the Lord, noth-ing in-deed shall I want.

1   The   Lord   is   my   shepherd;
2   He   guides   me   a - long   the   right   path;
3   You have pre -   pared   a   banquet   for   me
4   Surely   goodness   and   kindness   shall   follow me
5   To the   Father   and   Son   give   glory,

there   is   nothing   I   shall   want.
he   is   true   to   his   name.
in   the   sight   of   my   foes.
all   the   days   of   my   life.
give   glory   to   the   Spirit.

                Fresh   and   green   are   the   pastures
If I should   walk   in   the   valley   of   darkness
      My   head you have a - nointed   with   oil;
In   the   Lord's   own   house shall   I   dwell
To God who   is,   who   was,   and   who   will   be

where   he   gives   me   re - pose.   Near
       no   evil   would   I   fear.   You are

[——————————————
[——————————————
[——————————————

restful   waters   he   leads   me,
there   with   your   crook   and   your   staff;

——————————————]
——————————————]
——————————————]

to   re - vive   my   droop - ing   spir   -   it.
with   these   you   give   me   com   -   fort.
my   cup   is   o   - ver - flow   -   ing.
for   ev   -   er   and   ev   -   er.
for   ev   -   er   and   ev   -   er.

THROUGH-COMPOSED

The term "through-composed" is commonly misunderstood. It refers to psalm settings rendered by cantor or choir alone. More commonly, this method is combined with another method of rendition, the responsorial form. The intention of the composer is to find music that duplicates the emotional content and literary structure of a specific text. The end result usually involves little or no repetition of musical material.

CANTILLATION

Cantillation is a kind of half-speech, half-song which is improvised by the cantor to a specific psalm text. This method predates Christianity. Traditionally, there have been rules or guidelines for such improvisation. These might include the mode or key of a piece, as well as certain standard formulas for pitch selection. Clearly, such "improvisation" was not intended to be entirely spontaneous. This method should only be attempted by advanced cantors, and only after careful preparation.

MIXED

The combination of various methods is referred to as "mixed mediums." This might also designate the recitation of psalm text to an instrumental accompaniment with a sung refrain.

Ways of Singing the Psalms Without a Cantor

ANTIPHONAL

The antiphonal method of psalm singing requires that the assembly be divided into two groups (one may be the choir). The groups take turns in singing equal portions of the psalm, usually to the same melody. This melody is often a formula or psalm tone as described above. A refrain may be sung by all at the beginning and end of the psalm.

METRICAL

Sometimes psalms are given metrical settings. The psalm is organized into stanzas, with each stanza sung to the same notes and rhythms. In order to accomplish this, the psalm is usually paraphrased (at the risk of diminishing some of the original content). The entire psalm is sung by everyone. This method is also referred to as the "hymn" model. A good example is the hymn "All people that on earth do dwell," a paraphrase of Psalm 100. Liturgical law forbids the use of metrical psalmody where a psalm is indicated. Metrical psalms are suitable for various processions in the liturgy.

Both antiphonal and metrical forms are common in Protestant worship.

Other Cantor Repertory

The cantor has responsibility for any songs and hymns which require the rendering of solo passages. These pieces often give the assembly a recurring refrain to sing, with intervening sung statements or verses by the cantor. Thus they resemble the responsorial psalmody already discussed and the litanies described below. In some cases, the assembly sings a refrain continuously with the cantor's verses sung simultaneously in an "overlay" fashion. This is called an ostinato refrain.

LITANIES

A litany is a prayer of a repetitive nature with very frequent alternation between leader and assembly. It may accompany a ritual action such as the breaking of the bread ("Lamb of God") or the procession to the font (litany of the saints). The church has many litany prayers; those which follow should be familiar to every cantor.

Texts "Based on" Psalms

Texts described as "based on" certain psalms abound. Such a piece might be a paraphrase of a psalm, or it might simply be inspired by a psalm. For liturgical use, cantors and all who prepare the liturgy should respect the approved translations. In the United States these include the New American Bible, the Jerusalem Bible, the Revised Standard Version and the Grail Psalter. The greatest problem with these translations is the noninclusive language; this is being addressed by efforts toward revised translations.

Most of the "based on" texts are clearly inferior to the psalms themselves. Even when the text and music are both done well, these compositions should be sparingly used and should never be used as substitutes for the psalms themselves at their assigned places in the liturgy. In particular, the psalms alone—in their approved translations—are worthy of use after the first reading at Mass.

A useful resource for understanding and praying psalm texts is *Praying the Psalms* by Walter Brueggemann (Saint Mary's Press, 1982).

In the litany of the penitential rite the presider, deacon or cantor may call upon Jesus very simply as "Lord" or "Christ," or by various names or descriptions ("Lord, you bring glad tidings to the poor"). The presider, deacon or cantor concludes the statement with "Lord (Christ), have mercy." The people respond, echoing the words of the leader.

The "Lamb of God" litany accompanies the breaking of bread. The sacramentary says that this litany should be prolonged all through the breaking of the bread. The cantor may call upon Christ by various descriptive names, always beginning and ending with "Lamb of God." Other titles might include "Bread of life," "Prince of peace," and other scriptural images. The people respond each time with "Have mercy on us" and conclude with "Grant us peace."

The general intercessions or "prayer of the faithful" are a litany in which the deacon or cantor calls out the petitions for the church, the world, the oppressed and the local community. The people may respond to each intention: "Lord, have mercy" or "Lord, hear our prayer." The urgency of these prayers may be intensified by overlapping the leader's prayer or invitation and the assembly's response.

In the litany of the saints the cantor names or invokes the saints. The people respond to each invocation: "Pray for us." It is important that the flow of invocation and response is continuous; a litany does its work by catching everyone in its rhythm so that we are freed for complete immersion in the very sound of prayer. Other litanies in this format include the litany of Loreto (litany of the Blessed Virgin), the litany of the Holy Name, and the litany of St. Joseph.

GOSPEL ACCLAMATIONS

Gospel acclamations are another important part of cantor repertory. Outside of the lenten season, the alleluia is sung before the proclamation of the gospel. During Lent, one of the following acclamations is sung.

> Praise and honor to you, Lord Jesus Christ.
> Glory and praise to you, Lord Jesus Christ.
> Glory to you, word of God, Lord Jesus Christ.
> Praise to you, Lord Jesus Christ, king of endless glory.

The appropriate verse to accompany the gospel acclamation on a specific day can be found in the lectionary. This verse is sung by the cantor. The accompaniment editions of most Roman Catholic hymnals and missalettes offer settings of the gospel acclamations and corresponding tones for the recitation of the cantor's verse. The gospel acclamation with its verse is intended to accompany the procession; both music and procession then lead directly to the proclamation of the gospel. The sacramentary is clear that the gospel acclamation is to be sung; when for some reason this cannot be done, the acclamation is omitted.

GLORIA

The Gloria may also be a part of cantor repertory if sung alternately with the assembly. Such settings have been written to make musical rendition of this difficult and lengthy text more accessible.

PROCLAMATIONS

The cantor should also be familiar with various proclamations which are designated for certain times in the church's year. The Christmas and Epiphany proclamations can be found in the annual *Sourcebook for Sundays and Seasons* (Liturgy Training Publications). The Easter proclamation (Exsultet) can be found in the sacramentary. It is sung at the Easter Vigil and is the only proclamation designated as a part of the liturgy. The traditional Exsultet is a lengthy song of praise set to chant. It is difficult to execute and can be difficult to listen to if poorly done. Though assigned to the deacon, it may also

---

Acclamations

The acclamations of the eucharistic prayer belong first and foremost to the entire assembly. Rare occasions may call for music which requires a cantor for these acclamations such as a one-time gathering of people who have no common repertory. The execution of eucharistic acclamations in a "call and response" fashion is a teaching tool; it should not be used once the assembly has learned these parts of the liturgy.

be sung by a cantor. The decision should be based upon ability: Who can sing it in a way worthy of its poetry and message?

Musical, Liturgical, Pastoral

In selecting music for liturgical celebration from the overall repertory available, three judgments should be kept in mind. These are the musical judgment, the liturgical judgment and the pastoral judgment. Though often not the person to select music, the cantor should still know why certain pieces are being used. The informed cantor can better serve the assembly. Every cantor should read (and reread) *Music in Catholic Worship* and *Liturgical Music Today*. These brief documents were prepared by the Bishops' Committee on the Liturgy as vital guidelines and directives for the church in the United States. The importance and application of these three judgments is explained in *Music in Catholic Worship.*

The Cantor in Liturgical Celebration

Preparation

Music must be learned and rehearsed before the cantor arrives at church for a liturgy. The rehearsal should be with the instrumentalists, preferably in the worship space. There is not time to learn music or to rehearse adequately immediately prior to a liturgy. As a cantor, you also have to prepare in other ways. Here are some suggestions for preparation on the day of a liturgy.

Allow at least 15 minutes for vocal warm-up (vocalization), more if possible. This can take place at home or at church if space is available. Even your parked car can be used. Always begin with gentle vocalization, such as humming. Then vocalize using your most beautiful vowel sounds in the best part of your range (the best sounding and most easily produced notes in your voice). If you have the time, sing through all of the material you will be using for the day's liturgy. At the very least, sing through any spots which you found to be tricky or difficult when you learned and rehearsed the material. Read through the texts so that their content is uppermost in your mind.

Your attire for the day will depend primarily upon the expectation of the assembly. You should be neutral, in the sense that what you wear should not distract from what you are about. Keep in mind that it is your task to serve God by serving the assembly. If your attire sets you apart from the assembly because you are overdressed or underdressed, you may find it more difficult to perform your ministry.

Arrive at least 15 minutes before you are to begin. If you are going to introduce new material to the assembly, to review material or simply to warm up their voices, you may need to arrive earlier. Check in with any other musicians involved and with the presider in order to confirm plans. Clarify any questions regarding the day's liturgy.

While it is important to make last-minute preparations and to greet others, you should allow ample time to quiet yourself for the liturgy. Be particularly conscious that presiders and others are also trying to prepare; give them the space to do so. This is not a good time to make changes or suggestions, to try something spontaneously, or to conduct any kind of business that might be handled at another place and time. You should discreetly set up music and check your microphone at least ten minutes before you are to begin. This preparation should never take place after the people have begun to assemble. When people are running around and making last-minute adjustments right up to the beginning of worship, there is an atmosphere of a performance. This is simply disrespect for the assembly. Carefully timed preparation will make you feel good about what you are doing, and that feeling will be communicated to the assembly.

If all preparations are made in good time, you can relax and greet a few people in the assembly, then quiet yourself for the liturgy. The purpose of this is to block out any distractions and to allow you to enter fully into the liturgy, even as you perform this public ministry.

The place from which you sing is important. It is essential for you to be *seen* by the assembly. At the same time, it is important for you to be within working distance of any instrumentalists with whom you will be singing. Both of these are not always possible if the organ (console or pipes) is in a rear gallery. In that case you can work from the front with unaccompanied repertory, or other instruments, situated near you, can be used for accompaniment. A cantor should never be a solo voice emanating from the choir loft.

How to Prepare on Liturgy Days

Dress appropriately.
Vocalize.
Arrive early.
Check in with other musicians and with the presider.
Briefly greet others.
Set up music and check the microphone.
Quiet yourself.

Teaching Music to the Assembly

You will occasionally need to introduce new or less familiar material to the assembly prior to the liturgy. Specifics of how this should be done, and how frequently, should be decided by those in charge of music in consultation with others involved in the liturgy.

Be concise. What you are going to say should be written out and perhaps committed to memory. Always have the text before you as a safeguard. Failure to prepare a text usually leads to using too many words.

Be certain to speak clearly and distinctly. If you are nervous, you might tend to speak too rapidly or too quietly. Fight these inclinations. Believe that what you have to say is important and convey that feeling to the assembly. Speak deliberately.

Your ability to use a microphone well is important. Always practice beforehand (without the assembly present) to find the right distance from which to speak and to sing. Generally this is no less than six inches from the microphone and no more than twelve, but it will vary according to the type of microphone, the volume at which the microphone is set, and the acoustics of the church. If six inches from the microphone is still not loud enough, do not move in closer to increase volume. Instead, use your ability to project. Keep in mind that you are addressing a group of people and not speaking intimately with a single individual.

Preparatory Reflection

Sit down at your place. Close or lower your eyes, and breathe deeply. Breathe slowly and rhythmically. Block out any distractions and focus on how you feel, physically and emotionally. If there are any unpleasant feelings—tiredness, nervousness, concerns—try to let go of them by focusing on your breathing.

Next, try to focus on something uplifting. This might be a psalm or song from the day's liturgy or a reflection on the love of God. If it helps you to think of a specific prayer, savor each word and phrase. Otherwise, simply pray in your own words, in your own way. Reflect on why you are there and what it means to serve. (A good resource for such prayer is the book *Prayers of Those Who Make Music* [Liturgy Training Publications]. It can easily be tucked into a purse or pocket, making it readily available for personal reflection or shared prayer.)

Come back to the present by again becoming aware of the assembly. Look around you. Identify your pain and joy with that of these people.

When introducing or reviewing music before a liturgy, the piece itself and your chosen method of introduction will play a large part in determining your text. For a short refrain it may be enough to have the instrumentalist(s) play the refrain, to sing it yourself, and then to have the assembly sing it. It might be stated something like this:

> Good morning. (pause) Today and in the coming weeks we will be singing a refrain which may be unfamiliar to some of you. It can be found in _____ on page _____. Please follow along as I sing through it and then repeat after me.

After the music is sung, this introduction might continue with a statement of how or where the refrain is to be used. Conclude with a simple thank-you.

If the piece is longer, or more complex, you might begin by reading the text aloud while the assembly follows along. This is also a good way to highlight the text and to get people involved in its content. Do not read through many stanzas of a lengthy hymn as a way of teaching it to the assembly, but a few stanzas can be read. If you love the words and handle them well, your delight will be catching. As an example, imagine how you would read this text:

> Love divine, all loves excelling,
> Joy of heav'n, to earth come down!
> Fix in us thy humble dwelling,
> All thy faithful mercies crown.
> Jesus, thou art all compassion,
> Pure unbounded love thou art;
> Visit us with thy salvation,
> Enter ev'ry trembling heart.

Speaking to the Assembly

Your tone should be cordial and persuasive. Imagine that you are greeting friends whom you care for deeply. Isn't this really the case?

Write a thank-you note to a person or persons. Read it aloud. Use that same warmth when addressing the assembly.

When practicing with a microphone, speak and sing as if it were not there or were not functioning. Your voice will have more energy and intensity.

Be careful not to pop "b" or "p" when speaking and singing into the microphone. This will probably not happen unless you are too close.

Come, almighty, to deliver,
Let us all thy life receive;
Suddenly return and never,
Never more thy temples leave.
Thee we would be always blessing,
Serve thee as thy hosts above,
Pray, and praise thee without ceasing,
Glory in thy precious love.

Finish then thy new creation,
Pure and spotless let us be;
Let us see thy great salvation
Perfectly restored in thee!
Changed from glory into glory,
Till in heav'n we take our place,
Till we cast our crowns before thee,
Lost in wonder, love, and praise.

This text by Charles Wesley comes from his collection *Redemption Hymns* of 1747. Reading hymns such as this might help people to embrace texts and to think of hymns in their entirety.

A wonderful way to teach hymns or longer refrains is a method known as "lining-out." A piece is executed continuously, one phrase at a time. Each phrase is sung by the cantor and repeated immediately by the assembly. In the following example the cantor sings the hymn four measures at a time, with the people immediately repeating each phrase.

The stanza may then be sung in its entirety by all.

There are many ways to introduce or review music with the assembly. What is essential is that the language is clear and hospitable, that the introduction is carefully executed, and that you, the cantor, believe in what you are doing and asking the assembly to do. This is not the time to condescend ("After I sing for you, *please* try to repeat the refrain!"), to entertain ("You'll really love this one!"), or to chastise ("You're not singing!").

You should hope for a wholehearted response, but should not feel disappointed if the response is less than enthusiastic. Some people are slow to respond and others may never participate. Have a consistent approach and go for the long haul. In this regard, sound liturgical practice would demand that once a parish has found and learned music of quality, this should be used through a season or over several weeks of Ordinary Time. Those pieces which are used only in Lent, for example, should be used throughout Lent and year after year. A piece used only once a year (at the washing of feet, for example) should be used each year. This continuity, when the music itself is worthy, shows respect for the assembly and the liturgy. Often, music ministers tire of a piece long before the assembly. This is because they have much greater exposure to the music through continued practice and multiplication of liturgical celebrations. Try to approach familiar music in fresh, new ways.

Physical Communication and Animation of the Assembly

Gestures are an important part of inviting people to sing. As you sing, your arms should hang at your sides. If you must hold your music, you will be limited to one arm for your gestures; use a music stand that is serviceable and not obtrusive. When it is time for the assembly to sing, breathe with them. As you do so, raise your arms—with palms turned upward—to about shoulder height. The position should resemble one you would use to embrace someone. Let your arms remain in this position for a few seconds, and then let them fall slowly to their original position at your sides.

Introductions

Choose a hymn or refrain and write out several different introductions for it. Read each one aloud. Try to discern which introduction is the best by asking the following questions: Is the language hospitable? Is it concise? Is there ample opportunity for the assembly to listen and respond?

Another visual cue, raising of the eyes to take in the assembly, should accompany any gesture. In some cases, raising the eyes or nodding the head is a sufficient indication for people to sing. Some assemblies will sing enthusiastically with no physical cue at all. The point is that every cantor should be comfortable with gestures; the

Making Gestures

Choose a refrain with which to practice your gestures. Sing through the refrain as if you were intoning it for the assembly. Inhale, and raise your arms (and your eyes, if they have been buried in the music) as if cuing the singing of the assembly. Sing the refrain again and cue the imaginary assembly without using arms and hands. Try again using only one hand. Do this with refrains that begin on a variety of beats and fractions of beats, being certain that the gesture immediately precedes the singing of the assembly.

use of gestures will then be determined by the needs of the assembly and *not* by the limitations of the cantor.

It will not always be possible for the cantor to breathe with the assembly. Sometimes there is an overlap between the cantor's part and the people's response. In such a case the gesture must still precede the entrance of the assembly as described earlier, but without the actual intake of air by the cantor.

Body language in general should be attended to very carefully. You need to appear confident, but not cocky. If you fidget or avoid the eyes of those around you, you will make the assembly uncomfortable. If you come on like gangbusters, the members of the assembly might compensate by withdrawing. You should not be overly casual in your demeanor, nor should you be stiff or affected. It also helps to smile, if you can be natural doing so.

Move into position deliberately, but without haste. Do not move before you need to move. Your chair should be close enough to your music stand and microphone that you do not have to walk far. Remember that your movement sets an atmosphere for worship. It should have a certain dignity. When you have finished singing something, wait a moment before sitting down. You do not want to give the impression that you cannot wait for this to end. If you seem impatient, others will become impatient.

Like all members of the assembly, your attention should always be with what is happening in the liturgy. Try not to daydream, fuss with your music, hum or audibly clear your throat.

When you are singing before the assembly, be careful not to make extraneous movements, especially movements in time with the music. This will distract the assembly from what you are trying to express. Do not sway from side to side, rock back and forth, rise up on your toes, or squat on bent knees. Never use your hands to check for a tense throat, neck or jaw. Never cup your ear in order to hear yourself with greater clarity. Do not conduct in time to the music or strike affected poses, such as hands clasped before you. Many such movements are

---

Observing Others

Make a point of observing other cantors, lectors and presiders. Take note of both positive and negative aspects of their body language. Are there superfluous motions and gestures? Are deliberate gestures big enough to be seen? Are they overwhelming? Does the person appear confident? Why, or why not? What effect does eye contact from the person have on you? Does the minister have any special affectation?

done unconsciously, so that you may need to rely on the observations of others. Practice in front of a mirror to eliminate these and other physical idiosyncrasies.

It is not improper to sing with the assembly as a way of encouraging their singing and as a way of fulfilling your own role as a member of the assembly, but your voice should never overpower the singing of the assembly. If an organ is used, it should be the organ which leads and sustains the singing of the assembly. If other instruments are used, they should be capable of leading the assembly. Too often the cantor ends up singing in place of the assembly. If your own singing is amplified over the singing of the assembly, some may feel inclined to listen passively. Others may feel defeated and decide that their singing is unimportant. If you are singing at a microphone, step back or step aside when it is the assembly's turn to sing. It is easy to be seduced by the sound of your own voice. Strive to hear and to love the singing of the assembly.

Dealing with the Unexpected

Unexpected situations can arise in the course of a liturgy. Everything should be done to prevent such situations, but when they occur they should be handled calmly, with common sense and always with mutual charity.

When a microphone seems to fail, do not fidget with the microphone or its cord. If there is an on-off switch, look to see that it is on. Do not tap the mike or blow into it. If your singing is well focused, it will project without electronic amplification. Never let the assembly know that there is a problem. The story is told about a presider who announced to the assembly, "There is something wrong with this microphone," to which they responded, "And also with you."

If you make a mistake, do not panic. Everyone makes mistakes. Do what needs to be done and go on. Do not draw attention to your mistakes by getting mad, upset, or silly. These are things which might

---

Cantor and Assembly

Ask yourself the following hard questions. When the singing of the assembly is strong, do I get louder in order to be heard above it? Am I so certain that the assembly will not sing that I sing their parts for them—right into the microphone? Do I attempt to control the tempo of congregational singing, hoping the organist will follow? Do I enjoy the singing of the assembly, or am I impatient until it is my turn to sing alone?

come through in your body language if you are not in control. Similiarly, do not show anger or dismay because of objects which malfunction, babies who cry, or people who are unresponsive.

Never act judgmentally toward other liturgical ministers or members of the assembly. If the presider forgets that the Gloria is to be sung—even if the presider deliberately decides it should be recited—do not publicly show that anything is wrong. If a lector begins to recite a psalm when you have spent hours singing that psalm, let it go. Such matters can be calmly addressed after the liturgy. Never reprimand or chide the assembly for their apparent lack of involvement or for poor singing. Uncharitable behavior can only undermine what a cantor is about. Furthermore, people will be more likely to show charity toward you if you act in kind.

Evaluation

After the liturgy, make note of things which went wrong between you and other liturgical ministers. Ask the following questions.

Was there adequate preparation?

Rehearsal?

Communication?

Cooperation?

What might be done to avoid mistakes in the future?

Do not confront other ministers immediately after the liturgy. Find some time during the week to sit down and calmly discuss your concerns. Liturgical ministers are as human and fragile as anyone else. The last thing anyone needs is an "instant analysis" of their performance.

The Eucharistic Liturgy

Up to this point principles have been set forth which could be applied to any liturgical celebration. It is perhaps beneficial to look more specifically at the eucharistic liturgy.

Introductory Rites

The introductory rites of the liturgy always include the sign of the cross, the greeting and the opening prayer. The introductory rites may also include a gathering song, the blessing and sprinkling of water or the penitential rite, and the Gloria (outside of Advent and Lent). These elements work together to prepare the assembly, as a community, to hear the word and to celebrate the eucharist. The whole introductory rite should have a flow and pacing which goes beyond a succession of rubrics. Music should be an integral element of the introductory rites and not a decorative addition to it.

For an opening hymn or gathering song your role will depend upon several things. Is this piece sung in its entirety by the assembly? Is this a song or hymn which might require special animation? Does the song or hymn have musical passages requiring a cantor?

As for the remainder of the opening rites, you need only be prominent for pieces requiring the rendering of solo passages by a cantor. This might include the litany of the penitential rite or a setting of the Gloria sung in alternation with the assembly. There might also be a song for the sprinkling rite (which sometimes replaces the penitential rite). Many recent compositions for this rite need a cantor.

Care should be taken in selecting music for these rites. Music is essential, but failure to understand and respect the nature of the entrance rite can sometimes lead to "overload": too much unrelated music. The whole movement of the liturgy until the opening prayer is finished should have clarity and unity.

Liturgy of the Word

The liturgy of the word requires careful timing and pacing. It usually comprises:

- reading from the Hebrew Scriptures
- psalm
- reading from the letters of the New Testament
- gospel acclamation
- reading from the gospels
- homily
- creed
- prayers of intercession

During the first reading your full attention should be on the lector. When the lector has finished, wait. A period of silence is called for after each of the first two readings. Your parish should implement some standard way to carry this out. In many cases it will be up to you to determine the length of the silence. The instrumentalist will not begin the psalm until you are ready. Allow time for the lector to be seated and allow more time for reflective silence. All cantors should agree on the length of this silence. Then move deliberately, but without haste, to the place from which you will sing. The most common musical rendition of the responsorial psalm begins with an instrumental statement of the refrain, an intonation by the cantor, and its repetition by the entire assembly. All of the psalm verses given in the lectionary should be sung. (In many cases these are not entire psalms but verses selected for liturgical use.) When you have finished, do not run away. Wait just a moment and then calmly return to your place.

The same approach to silence holds true for timing the gospel acclamation. Allow time after the second reading before moving into position. In some parishes the cue comes from the presider or the instrumentalist. All should be clear about the length of the silence and the cue for the acclamation. It will not usually be necessary to gesture for the assembly to stand, but use a gesture if needed. As soon as the gospel acclamation has concluded, perhaps even earlier, direct your attention to the book and the gospel reader. Listen attentively to this proclamation of the word. Do not bother with your music until the gospel has concluded and it is time for all to be seated. Then the action of the entire assembly will cover any movement you need to make. As with the readings, be attentive to the homily.

Do not compete with the presider or the assembly in the recitation of the creed (or the recitation of any part of the liturgy). These are intended to be spoken in unison by the entire assembly. While cantors and other liturgical ministers should enthusiastically participate, they must be careful not to overwhelm the assembly. Their voices should not be picked up by the microphones and amplified.

The general intercessions can and often should be sung. Care must be taken by those who write the prayers that they are not too long or too wordy. Pacing is again important. These prayers should have a sense of urgency, and the assembly's response should flow from the intercessions. (As mentioned earlier, an overlap between the leader's invitation and the assembly's response can be very effective.)

Liturgy of the Eucharist

The liturgy of the eucharist begins with the preparation of the gifts and continues through the eucharistic prayer and the communion rite. The communion rite comprises the Lord's Prayer, the sign of peace, the "Lamb of God" litany, the communion, and the prayer after communion. Care must be taken that the lesser elements do not overpower the eucharistic prayer and the communion.

The preparation of the gifts is not an ideal time for singing by the assembly. Instrumental music can help the assembly rest a bit from all the words which are a necessary part of the liturgy. Furthermore, there is considerable activity taking place. In addition to the preparation of the gifts, a collection may be taken. It only complicates matters to attempt a hymn or song. This is not a portion of the liturgy which should be highlighted.

After the preparation of the gifts, the liturgy of the eucharist continues with the eucharistic prayer, the core of the entire liturgy. You should be attentive and participatory during the eucharistic prayer, but it is not necessary or even preferable to stand at the microphone. Respond as a member of the assembly when the presider leads the preface dialogue. Even if this is sung, it should not be necessary for you to lead the assembly's responses; your presence and amplified voice will only distract from the liturgical focus. If the musical setting is known by the assembly and not changed too often, the assembly should respond well.

The assembly's acclamations to the eucharistic prayer are the "Holy, holy," the memorial acclamation and the great Amen. If you have been singing these acclamations into a microphone for some time, allow ample time for a successful change. If after some weeks the assembly is still not responsive, consider the source of the problem. Is the instrumental leadership adequate? Is the tempo steady and well suited to the setting? Are the instruments loud enough? Are they too loud? Are the presider and other liturgical ministers participatory? Are the musical settings too difficult? Are they in too high a key? Are they stale or trite? Is the room so poor acoustically that it is not possible to hear the singing of the assembly, or for them to hear each other?

The "Our Father" may be sung, but the setting should be accessible to all. A song is not appropriate during the sign of peace. An exception might be made from time to time, but this should not become a regular practice. Everything in the communion rite should lead to the communion procession. Again, there is a risk in highlighting too many lesser moments: the most significant points in the liturgy will be diminished.

The "Lamb of God" litany should be sung. It begins as the presider starts to break the bread and it should last until the breaking of the bread and the preparation of the wine are completed. This litany can be especially effective if linked instrumentally to the communion song. It is most important that the communion song begin promptly after the people's response, "Lord, I am not worthy . . ."

The very nature of the communion procession calls for song by the assembly. It is most practical to use a refrain form. This enables people to sing without the hindrance of books. The cantor should not feel intrusive or be reluctant to lead. Now is the time for people to be aware of those around them, to be aware of the church here nourished at the common table by the body and blood of Christ. Song is an integral part of our communion: It is a natural accompaniment to the procession, an audible presence of brothers and sisters to one another, a source of insight into the mystery in which we share. During communion some will be waiting to receive communion, some will be focused on the words of the eucharistic ministers and some will already have received communion. The action of the whole can be unified by a single, well-chosen communion song. The communion song might be extended by instrumental verses, by doubling the refrain each time it is sung, or by simple repetition.

If two songs are used, they might be woven together in some musical way. At the very least they should be musically and textually compatible. Two very different styles of music may be very compatible depending upon key and melodic content. For example:

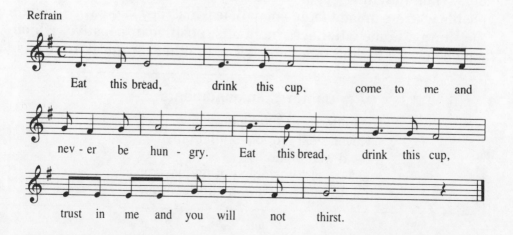

Music in Catholic Worship is very specific about what the content of the communion song is to be or not to be.

> The communion song should foster a sense of unity. It should be simple and not demand great effort. It gives expression to the joy of unity in the body of Christ and the fulfillment of the mystery being celebrated. Because they emphasize adoration rather than communion, most benediction hymns are not suitable. In general, during the most important seasons of the church year—Easter, Lent, Christmas, and Advent—it is preferable that most songs used at the communion be seasonal in nature. For the remainder of the church year, however, topical songs may be used during the communion procession, provided these texts do not conflict with the paschal character of every Sunday.   (#62)

After communion it is possible to have a song or hymn of thanksgiving, or one of a more reflective nature. This may or may not employ cantor. Before choosing to add a song at this point, motives should be carefully considered. Is this something that will contribute in a significant way to the community's celebration or will it merely satisfy some special interest?

The communion rite (and the liturgy of the eucharist) concludes with the prayer after communion spoken or sung by the presider.

Concluding Rite

The liturgy concludes with the blessing and dismissal. If a closing song is sung, it is preferable that all the ministers (including the presider) remain in place and sing at least some of the song. Do not expect the assembly to stay and sing after the liturgical ministers have left. If there is a formal procession, music should accompany the movement. If the hymn is not long enough, the music can be extended instrumentally.

If the hymn requires no solo singing on your part, you may process with the other ministers or you may remain as a part of the assembly. When the liturgy is over you may want to linger a little. Often, people who are unfamiliar to you will feel that they know you through the liturgy. Some will have comments, positive or negative, which may be useful to you, other musicians or other liturgical ministers.

Cantor Commandments

Be attentive to the liturgy.
Never steal the focus from others.
Lead with authority.
Listen for the singing of the assembly.
Participate fully and enthusiastically.

For Further Reading on Liturgical Celebration

Tad Guzie, *The Book of Sacramental Basics* (New York: Paulist Press, 1981). 140 pages. Offers insight into the meaning of the sacraments.

Gabe Huck, *Liturgy with Style and Grace* (Chicago: Liturgy Training Publications, 1984). 131 pages. Basic guide to liturgical celebration: liturgical ministers, the liturgical year, components of the eucharistic liturgy.

Aidan Kavanagh, *Elements of Rite* (New York: Pueblo Publishing Company, 1982). 109 pages. "A Handbook of Liturgical Style," with basic guidelines for troubleshooting.

The Liturgy Documents, A Parish Resource, edited by Mary Ann Simcoe (Chicago: Liturgy Training Publications, 1985). 320 pages. The most significant liturgy documents of the church.

The Cantor As a Singer

Good Habits

This section deals with basic aspects of singing. Beginning and advanced cantors alike should have a fundamental knowledge of their vocal instrument and they should apply that knowledge to their singing. This will make it much easier to pinpoint and resolve vocal problems; it may even prevent serious problems from developing.

A cantor should practice daily and must be willing to abandon personal inhibition in the pursuit of vocal skill. Vocal study should not be confused with the cultivation of an ''operatic'' voice. Folk singers, pop singers, singers of art songs—as well as those who sing opera—all require training and practice in order to develop the beauty, control and consistency that will allow them to communicate in their chosen idiom. Of course, any highly stylized approach is to be avoided by the cantor. Sometimes performers go out of their way to develop a style which sets them apart or makes a statement. Such an approach by the cantor will diminish the power of texts and may even exclude certain members of the assembly from participation.

You have probably been surprised by the sound of your own voice as captured on a tape. This is because it is not possible to sing or to speak and at the same time to listen to your own voice objectively. We all need other ears to trust for criticism and evaluation of our voices. Tape recordings can be useful, but there are times when a singer must rely on the immediate perception of others. Seek out a teacher, coach or colleague for this purpose.

Good physical health is essential to good singing. Proper diet and adequate rest are fundamental. Develop a routine of adequate sleep, with a consistent time for rising and retiring. Extremes of weight in one direction or the other can be a great hindrance to singing. Singers should strive for a moderate weight and should be engaged in some kind of aerobic exercise, no matter how basic. This will improve breathing and will help to develop stamina.

Obviously, singers should not smoke. Caffeine and alcohol are to be avoided since both of these dehydrate the body and the latter can cause swelling of the vocal bands. Hydration is very important to good singing. In dry weather you may find it helpful to drink as many as ten glasses of water a day.

Singers should be cautious about singing with a cold or any other virus. The vocal apparatus can become tired and vulnerable to the body's infection. When recovering from a bad throat, use gentle vocalization such as humming for the first few days of practice. Never attempt to sing through pain or irritation. See a throat specialist if such a condition persists.

Singing is a physical activity and the muscles involved in singing should be exercised. The exercises provided below will offer a point of departure for various aspects of vocal development. Muscular responses should eventually become automatic. Muscle memory can only be affected through repetition and regular practice. Set aside a regular time for daily practice and keep it a priority. You will be rewarded with consistent results.

The basics of singing can be broken down into these categories: breathing (respiration), vocal production (phonation), vocal quality and projection (resonance), and articulation (the clear and distinct utterance of words). These will each be considered after an introductory section on posture.

Posture

Breathing is fundamental to singing and proper posture is fundamental to efficient breathing. Use a full-length mirror to check your posture; ask others to check you when performing or when no full-length mirror is available.

Standing with feet no more than shoulder's width apart, distribute your weight evenly between both feet, favoring the balls of your feet. Do not stand flat-footed or rock back on your heels. Your legs should be straight, but your knees should not be locked as this creates tension and can cut off circulation. Stand straight and tall from head to foot, but not rigidly. Your body should be relaxed but not limp. Strive for a feeling of readiness or pleasant anticipation. Imagine that something wonderful is about to happen (perhaps it will).

Raise your arms high over your head. Now lower them, keeping your chest high. Keep your back straight, not arched. Your arms should hang naturally at your sides. Your shoulders should be down and back, but in a comfortable position. Do not brace your shoulders back, but let them find the correct position through relaxation. Your neck and head should be straight and in alignment with the rest of the body. Be certain not to tilt the head to either side. Do not jut the head forward or pull it back. It should be balanced over the neck and torso.

Proper posture should be used in every possible situation so that it becomes completely natural and automatic. A mirror should be used to check posture from time to time, but the "feeling" of good posture must be memorized. To get the "feeling" of proper posture, lie down flat on your back on the floor. Make note of your body's alignment. Not only will proper posture help your singing, it will enhance your ability to communicate and help to build self-confidence.

Breathing

The mechanics of breathing are frequently misunderstood, particularly with regard to the diaphragm. The diaphragm is a dome-shaped muscular membrane attached to the lower portion of the rib cage. It acts as a partition between the organs of the chest and those of the abdomen. It is the primary muscle of inhalation but is not itself observable.

The diaphragm contracts for inhalation. When it is contracted, it flattens to a lower position, pushing the organs of the abdomen downward and the belly outward. This creates space in the chest cavity and a partial vacuum in the lungs, into which air is drawn. Take a quick, deep breath, as if surprised. Notice the expansion around your waist.

Tense?

To eliminate tension, gently roll shoulders forward several times, and then backward. Let your head drop forward, so that your chin is resting or almost resting on your chest. Slowly roll your head to the left, so that your left ear is toward your left shoulder. Slowly roll your head back to the center, and then to the right. Repeat this several times. Shake out any tension in your arms and legs.

The diaphragm relaxes for exhalation. The abdominal muscles assist the diaphragm in controlled relaxation. The abdominal muscles move inward for exhalation, but they should not collapse or be "squeezed" inward. The resistance of the abdominal muscles to an inward collapse is often referred to as "support." Take a deep breath, and let the air out slowly in a buzz, "zzzzz . . ." Maintain proper posture throughout, with special care to keep the chest high. Strive for absolute evenness and consistency of sound, without accents or interruptions in sound, and at one level of volume. Repeat the exercise. This time, try to exert a slight outward pressure at the waist while buzzing. The buzz should now have even greater consistency. If not, try lifting a heavy object while buzzing. This will cause the abdominal muscles to contract. The contraction of the abdominal muscles works in opposition to the relaxation of the diaphragm, assisting support.

In striving for support, the abdominal muscles must never become rigid or immobile. You must be able to relax, even go limp for inhalation. If these muscles tighten uncontrollably, try lying down and breathing deeply, as in sleep. Panting like a dog is another way to develop and maintain abdominal flexibility.

Breathe through your nose during long rests to avoid drying out. For short rests and between phrases, breathe through your mouth. This will allow you to take in a large breath quickly. The following exercises employ rests to assist in teaching proper breathing. Inhale quietly, without gasping. Keep your head and shoulders still for inhalation; check yourself in a mirror. Strive for deep, relaxed inhalation and maintain correct posture throughout.

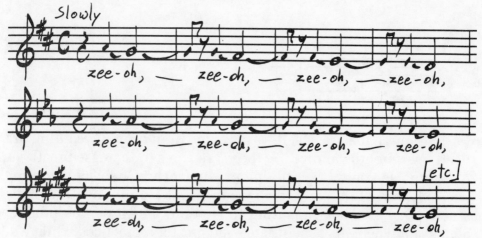

Of course, inhalation must be accomplished within the time allowed by the music. Where no rest is provided for a breath, it is a common error to hold a musical phrase out to its full duration, and then to take a breath before beginning the next phrase. This adds time to the phrase and seriously disturbs rhythmic flow. You should instead take a bit from the first in order to provide opportunity for a breath and still arrive on time for the next phrase.

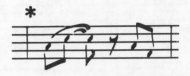

Although the greatest rewards come from proper breathing practiced over months and years, there are ways to increase breath supply or to use your air supply more efficiently. One way is to inhale and exhale rhythmically to a steady count (count silently). This is a good way to relate breathing to rhythm, and it can be practiced almost anywhere. Its benefits are even greater if practiced while walking. Begin by inhaling to a comfortable count of perhaps eight, and exhale to that same count. Then extend the count to something less comfortable. Do not speed up the count. Eventually the higher count will become comfortable and you will again need to extend the count.

Another way to increase or efficiently use your breath supply is to practice a long phrase by beginning near the end of it, gradually increasing the portion of the phrase which is sung until the entire phrase can be sung. Again, be careful not to speed up. You might even divide a long phrase into fractions. This will give you a goal for the expenditure of air (much like a budget).

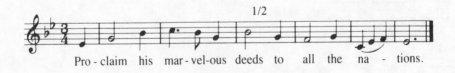

For ev - er I will sing the good-ness of the Lord.

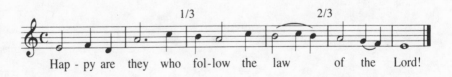

Pro - claim his mar - vel-ous deeds to all the na - tions.

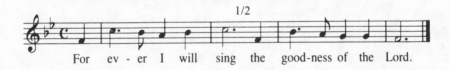

Hap - py are they who fol-low the law of the Lord!

Vocal Production

Sighing and humming are good ways to begin vocalization. The breath should cause the sound to begin. If the vocal chords are closed before exhalation has begun, pressure will build up behind them, causing them to open explosively. This is known as a glottal attack. It results in a much less pleasant sound and can be injurious to the voice over a period of time. To avoid the glottal attack, begin your sighing and humming with an "h" as in "hahhh" and "hmmm."

It is important to begin by warming up the most beautiful notes in your voice on the most beautiful vowels in your voice. Some people sound better singing "oh" and others "ee." Use a tape recorder and consult others to discover what your best vowel is. Begin a warm-up using your best vowel in order to establish a high quality of sound as the goal for all of your vowels. Start with a few consecutive notes in a comfortable part of your vocal range and work outward. The vowel [ē] as in "beet" and [ā] as in "paper" are particularly good for achieving clarity of sound. For rounding a sound which is perceived as strident and for adding depth to a thin sound, [ō] as in "oak" is very useful. These vowels should be sung with a pure, consistent vowel sound from beginning to end, unaffected by regional dialects.

When practicing a melody to be sung, it is often good to practice singing the entire piece on a single beautiful vowel. After returning to the text, notice which vowel sounds do not match the beauty of the others. Then practice the melody again, substituting a "good" vowel for the problem vowel. Try to substitute vowels which are similiar to your problem vowel. You might substitute [ō] as in "oak" for [ŏ] as in "hot," [ā] as in "paper" for [ĕ] as in "letter," [ē] as in

---

Breathing Checklist

Check for the following as you breathe for singing. You should be able to answer "yes" in every case.

Am I maintaining correct posture throughout?

Am I allowing my abdomen to move outward for inhalation? Am I keeping my head and shoulders still? Is my inhalation quiet? Am I inhaling within the time allowed by the music?

Am I able to keep my chest high during exhalation? Do my abdominal muscles resist sinking inward too quickly? When I sustain a tone, is it even in volume, tone quality and intonation?

"beet" for [ĭ] as in "will," or the reverse of any of these pairs. When you again return to the text, try to keep the tone quality of the substitute vowels.

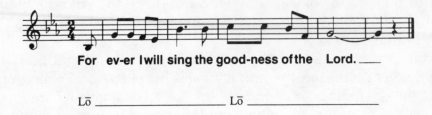

For ev-er I will sing the good-ness of the   Lord. ___

Lō _____ Lō _____

I will praise your name, my   King___ and my   God.

Zay _____ Zay _____

I will praise your name, my   King___ and my God.___

Zay _____ Zay _____

Most of what is involved in the sustaining of a tone can be related to proper breathing, but moving from one pitch to another on a single vowel presents other problems. This requires the smoothest possible connection of tones without sliding. It is a common error to aspirate a vowel when moving from one note to another. The substitution of [y] or [w] for the aspirate [h] may be practiced as a step in correcting this problem, but they must be eliminated for actual performance.

Practice the following exercises for smooth movement from one note to another.

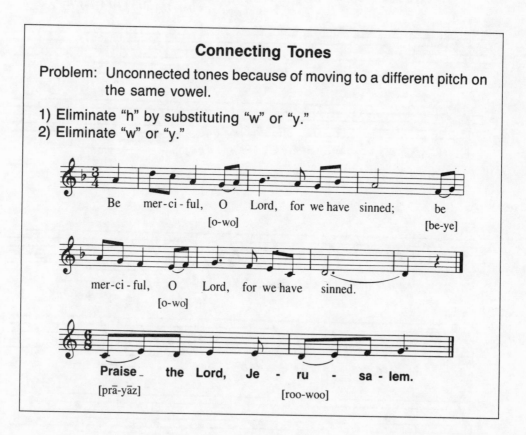

Connecting Tones

Problem: Unconnected tones because of moving to a different pitch on the same vowel.

1) Eliminate "h" by substituting "w" or "y."
2) Eliminate "w" or "y."

The release of a tone should be handled as carefully as the initiation of a sound. Closing the throat is the wrong way to end a tone. Instead, you may continue to exhale, but silently. You may also inhale at the end of a phrase to release a tone. This is a remedy for certain problems of articulation, such as the hissed sound of a final [s], and it prepares you for the next musical phrase.

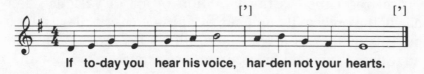

Note that each phrase ends in "s." Be certain to shorten the last note of the first phrase in each example, in order to provide time for the breath.

Vocal Quality and Projection

Personal taste plays a large role in the tone quality and volume we use for singing. We may imitate those singers we admire, or we may react to preconceived notions about ourselves as a certain "type" of singer. (Singers have been known to say such

---

Vocal Production Test

The following questions should be asked periodically, with regard to vocal production:

Do I begin singing vowels without a glottal attack? Do I end a tone with air? Do I end a tone with an inhalation?

Are all of my vowels becoming as beautiful as my best vowels? In other words, is my sound consistently beautiful? Am I extending my range of beautiful notes?

Can I move from one pitch to another on a single vowel with a smooth connection of tone, but without sliding?

things as "I'm an alto, so I can't sing those high notes," or "I can't sing very loud because I have a light voice.") The goal should always be the best sound for a given voice, recognizing that this is still highly subjective. As you practice, try to be open to new sounds in your voice. Do not be disappointed if you do not sound like your favorite recording artist. The beauty of a voice is its individuality.

Vocal resonance is the vibration of air in various chambers, primarily the oral cavity and surrounding areas. It plays a large part in the tone quality of a voice and allows for projection of a vocal sound. Space is needed for resonance to occur. Take a breath, inhaling quickly and deeply, as if surprised. Breathe through your nose and mouth simultaneously. The back of your tongue should be forward and out of your throat. Your throat should have a feeling of openness without being forced.

Try the exercise again. This time, exclaim "Oh!" immediately after the intake of air. The sound should be rich and full. Trying one last time, sing [o], as in "oak," immediately after the intake of air. Choose a note in the best part of your voice. Do not back away from the sound. If you have never made this kind of sound, you may be afraid of it, but it will become familiar over a period of time.

An inhibitor to good vocal quality is tension in the jaw and tongue. The lower jaw should hang freely from the face and the tongue lie flat in the mouth, with the tip of the tongue just behind the lower teeth. The following exercises should assist in relaxing the jaw and tongue:

- To make sure that the jaw is relaxed, wiggle it with your hand while practicing an exercise.

- Shake your head while singing, as if saying "no," and allow the jaw and tongue to be loose.

- Imagine a heavy weight hanging from your lower jaw that will not allow you to keep your teeth together.

- Make a "dopey" face or adopt a dumbfounded expression.

- Put your hands to the sides of your face to make certain that the back of the jaw is open and relaxed. (There may be tension in the back of the jaw even when the chin is down.)

- To loosen the jaw, exaggerate its movement and say or sing "yah, yah," "wah, wah," "blah, blah," or "gah, gah."

- While singing or humming, gently feel the area below your chin. Continue to feel this area without singing. If it bulges when you vocalize, the back of the tongue is stiff and pushed back into the throat. Gently push against this bulge while singing/humming, noting the difference in sound and feeling.

- Stick your tongue out as far as possible, and then slowly allow the tongue to return to its normal position, without allowing it to back into the throat.

- Roll the middle of your tongue forward, up and out of your mouth while keeping the tip down behind the lower teeth. This will give you the feeling of a forward tongue.

- You should be able to change from one vowel to another without moving the jaw. Relax the tongue and allow it to move for the change of vowel.

- Sing through the following exercise, watching in a mirror to ensure that the jaw does not move.

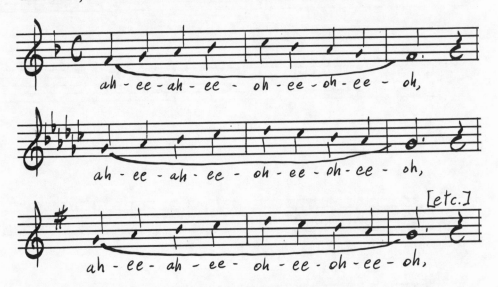

ah - ee - ah - ee - oh - ee - oh - ee - oh,

ah - ee - ah - ee - oh - ee - oh - ee - oh,

[etc.]

ah - ee - ah - ee - oh - ee - oh - ee - oh,

Some people think of vocal quality and projection as the "placement" of a voice. This is because of physical sensations related to singing, vibrations in the head, the chest or the face. You should strive for a forward placement, a feeling of vibrations in the front of the face and mouth. The following exercises should assist you:

- Hum and groan on [n] or [m].

- Imitate a siren on these same consonants.

- Pucker your lips while singing in a "fish mouth" which exposes both upper and lower front teeth.

- Imagine a wonderful, awful, or strange smell. Then keep that feeling while humming or singing.

- Sneer while singing (for practice only, please).

- Smile inwardly while singing (you may smile outwardly, as well, but not too "tightly").

Articulation

As Americans, we tend to be careless with the English language, even when singing or proclaiming the word of God. A refrain, such as "The Lord is kind and merciful," often sounds more like "The Lord is kinda merciful." The phrase, "The Lord is my help," takes on quite a different meaning if the final "p" is not carefully attended to.

It is essential that enough care be taken so that every word of every piece is clearly understood. There are many fine books which deal in depth with matters of articulation (for example, *The Singer's Manual of English Diction* by Madeleine Marshall, published by Schirmer books). For the purposes of this workbook, a few common problems will be addressed. The goal is always crisp, clear consonants and pure, sustained vowel sounds.

The first problem involves the differentiation between voiced consonants and unvoiced consonants. Voiced consonants are produced by the voice in coordination with the articulators (the lips, teeth and tongue): for example, [b], [d], [v], [g] and [z]. Unvoiced consonants are produced by the breath in coordination with the articulators, but *without* the sound of the voice, for example, [p], [t], [f], [k] and [s]. Pronounce these consonants, noting the differences between them. There must be distinct differentiation between [b] and [p], [d] and [t], [v] and [f], [g] and [k], [z] and [s], and other combinations of these voiced and unvoiced consonants.

Final consonants tend to be the most neglected of all because care is not taken to sing through to the end of a word. In the case of final [d], when not followed immediately by a word which begins with a vowel or by any word at all, it is necessary to add a shadow vowel in order for the [d] to be heard as a [d]. (Of course, there are exceptions. When the suffix -ed follows an unvoiced consonant, such as [k], it is pronounced [t]. "Looked" is pronounced "lookt.") In the phrase "Hear me, Lord," the word "Lord" should be pronounced "Lorduh" or "Lordih." This is necessary, but it should not be exag-

---

Quality and Projection Test

Ask yourself these questions:

Is my jaw relaxed?

Is my tongue relaxed and out of my throat?

Can I feel vibrations in my face and mouth when singing?

gerated. The "uh" or "ih" should barely be heard. Final [b] as in "Job" and hard [g] as in "beg" are treated the same as final [d], and are given a shadow vowel when not followed by a vowel sound. Read the following lines aloud:

I <u>beg</u> the <u>Lord</u> to forgive me.

<u>Job</u> <u>longed</u> to appear before <u>God</u>.

It is a common mistake to follow other voiced consonants in final position with a shadow vowel. This is unnecessary and only garbles text. "I will praise your name" becomes "I willuh praiseuh your nameuh." Simply sing through [l], [m], [n], [ng], [v] and [z], without adding anything. Shadow vowels are also not necessary or helpful when attempting to separate words for clarity. One presider was often heard to say, "Let usuh pray" in order to avoid "Let us spray." It would be better to make a slight stop between "us" and "pray."

Voiced and Unvoiced Consonants

Try speaking and singing the following pairs of words. Use a tape recorder and listen for careful distinction between them.

and — ant	deer — tier
have — half	bag — back
back — pack	plays — place
race — raise	God — cod
God — got	very — fairy
cheer — jeer	marching — margin
lags — lacks	moth — mother

Articulation Test #1

Tape yourself singing. Listen to the tape and ask yourself these questions.

When I sing, are final d's, b's and g's distinct?

Am I adding any unnecessary shadow vowels to the ends of words?

Do I make clear distinctions between voiced and unvoiced consonants?

Sometimes articulation is impaired because the singer diminishes volume on voiced consonants. It is important to sing/hum through voiced consonants with loose, relaxed lips and tongue. Carry the intensity of sound to the very ends of words and phrases. Sing the refrain "I will praise your name, my King and my God" on a single pitch. Carry the intensity of sound through final [l], [z], [m] and [ng].

It is also important to sing voiced consonants crisply and on one pitch only. Lingering too long over voiced consonants can give improper accents to certain words, and singing a voiced consonant on more than one pitch produces a "slide." Be particularly careful of lingering over [l], [m] and [n], especially when changing pitches. Sing the example below, taking care not to slide.

Sing the following, using the tip of the tongue and keeping the jaw still, but relaxed. (Use a mirror or your hand to check.) Consonants should be crisp and clean.

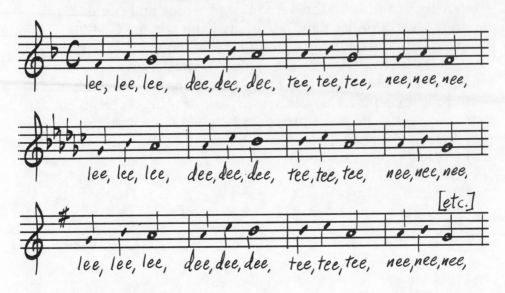

Repeat with other vowel sounds. Sing this next exercise with loose lips and minimal jaw movement.

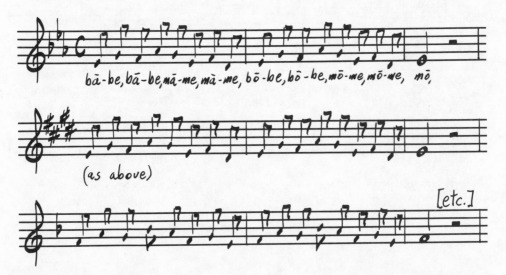

Singers are often told to sing on the vowel. Vowels sustain a vocal line. It is important not to diminish a vowel sound as it approaches a final consonant, or to allow the approaching consonant to modify the sound of the vowel. English has very few pure vowels, but many diphthongs. Diphthongs are two adjacent vowel sounds, such as the combination of ''ah'' and ''eee'' in the words ''I'' and ''mine.'' Both vowel sounds must be pronounced (or the result will resemble a Southern dialect), but the first should be held out as long as possible before singing the second. Of course, the second vowel sound should have the same intensity and volume as the first.

In the following musical examples, try singing the underlined diphthongs improperly, moving immediately to the second vowel sound, and then properly, singing on the first vowel sound until the last possible moment.

The_ Lord is my light and my sal - va - tion.

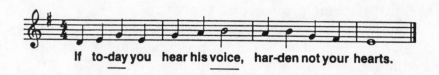

If to-day you hear his voice, har-den not your hearts.

I will praise your name for ev - er, _____ my

king and my God. _____

"d" and "n," "b" and "m"

Speak and sing the following pairs of words for differentiation.

door — nor	bore — more
day — nay	bay — may
dumb — numb	bum — mum
dud — done	dub — dumb
dear — near	mere — beer

The letter [r] presents special problems. When singing in Americanized English, you should use the American [r]. Suffice it to say that you should never roll or flip an [r], as Europeans do.

There are some times, however, when [r] should be completely omitted: for example, to avoid altering the quality of a vowel which precedes it. When [r] occurs before a consonant, as in "Lord," it does not need to be pronounced to be heard. It is implied. The vowel sound may be left exactly as it is when the [r] is spoken. The letter [r] is also omitted before a pause. An easy shorthand involves a slash through any [r] which is omitted, as in the following.

The Lord is kind and merciful.

An [r] should be sung before a vowel sound. It should be crisp, quick, and should not alter any preceding vowel sound, for example, "spirit" not "spirrrit." Pronounce such an [r] at the beginning of the next syllable, even when doubled, as in "sorrow" (spi-rit, sor-row). Just remember to sing on the vowel.

Study every text you are going to sing and practice reading each text aloud. Be certain of the correct pronunciation of every word; consult a dictionary if necessary. If your articulation is still unclear, try the following:

- Practice whispering the text. It will make you aware of the consonants.

- Sing the text staccato, with each word or syllable as short as possible. This will help you to execute quick consonants.

- Exaggerate your facial movement. This will loosen up the muscles of articulation.

- Sing exaggerated, loud consonants.

The Letter "r"

Practice speaking and chanting   singing the following phrases with careful attention to the pronunciation or elimination of [r].

Let all the earth cry out to God with joy.

Lord, send out your spi-rit, and renew the face of the earth.

Lord, you have the words of everlasting life.

If today you hear his voice, harden not your hearts.

Articulaton Test #2

Ask a friend or colleague to listen to you sing; pose the following questions:

Could you understand every word?

Did anything in the articulation of the text detract from its meaning or beauty?

For Further Reading on Vocal Pedagogy

Richard Alderson, *Complete Handbook of Voice Training* (West Nyack NY: Parker Publishing Company, 1979). 255 pages.

Ralph D. Appelman, *The Science of Vocal Pedagogy* (Bloomington IN: Indiana University Press, 1986). 448 pages.

Richard Rosewall, *Handbook of Singing* (Evanston IL: Dickerson Press, 1984). 84 pages.

William Vennard, *Singing: The Mechanism and the Technic* (New York: Carl Fischer, 1967). 275 pages.

These books offer various degrees of vocal science as well as practical exercises/techniques for singing.

I nterpretation

This section is for more advanced cantors, but some of the ideas presented will be accessible to the beginner. Incorporate what you can at your present level of ability and experience.

As a singer, you must interpret the words and music you sing in order for a piece to come to life. You must be able to convey the "essence" of a piece to the assembly. Of course not every assembly is the same and not every assembly should be addressed in the same way. Always keep the assembly in mind when interpreting a piece.

To interpret a piece you must discern the intentions of the author and the composer. If possible, research the text and the origins of both the text and the music. Begin with any information that is given on the page. Is this a psalm or scriptural quotation? Is it a prayer, an acclamation, a hymn of praise, or something else? Read the text carefully for its content. What is its subject matter? Sing the text. What is the mood? Is it the purpose of this work to console, to challenge, to inspire, to make petition, to lament, or simply to rejoice? Could it have more than one purpose?

Try to identify the following with regard to the text provided.

- origin of the text
- origin of the tune
- subject matter
- mood
- liturgical usage

Lord, You Raised Lazarus

LORD, YOU RAISED LAZARUS   Irregular with response*

TEXT: From the *Rite of Funerals* © 1970, International Committee on English in the Liturgy, Inc. (ICEL). All rights reserved.
TUNE: Laurence Bévenot, O.S.B., from *Music for Rite of Funerals and Rite of Baptism for Children* © 1977, ICEL, Inc. All rights reserved.

Another guide to the interpretation of a piece is its form, the form of both text and music. Begin with the obvious. Note any textual and musical repetitions, both literal and approximate. Is there a refrain? Do verses have ideas which run parallel? Is the music the same for each verse, merely related, or completely different? Does each phrase (musical and textual sentence) have the same number of measures? Note the phrase structure, as in the example below.

Also look at the music for delineations of sections by means of double bars, changes of tempo or meter, changes in intensity or dynamic, and changes in the instrumental parts.

Identify the textual and musical points of climax. Read the text aloud. Note the words and phrases in the text which are most important to its message. Underline these words in order to give them stress. In the music, look for extremes of melodic range and for notes emphasized by longer duration. Look for musical accents and for words and phrases emphasized by extremely loud or soft dynamics, or by sudden changes of volume. Note those places where the music best underscores the text.

Note the following in the example provided.

- repetitions/presence of a refrain
- similarity/dissimilarity between verses
- phrase structure
- double bar/change of key
- changes in volume
- high points in text and music

If you be-lieve in me you shall nev - er thirst.

At the most basic level of interpretation you must bring out important words and phrases. Once that has become comfortable, you are ready to deal with the interpretation of every word. Just as certain words will be emphasized, other words will be minimized, but there are more than two levels of inflection. Additionally, there are natural word accents. <u>Note</u> the <u>under</u>lined <u>words</u> and <u>syl</u>lables in <u>this</u> <u>sen</u>tence. Word accents are often undermined by singers. How many times have you heard someone sing "alleluia," simply because that syllable had a longer duration, was placed on the downbeat, or was given the highest or lowest pitch in a phrase?

Al - le - lu - ia,   al - le - lu - ia,   ₀ al - le - lu - ia.

Natural word accents must take precedence in order for the text to be clearly understood. Practice speaking any text you are going to sing, and strive for the same inflection when words and music are put together.

Word color is another way to enhance the interpretation of a text. It involves the nuance used to say or sing a text in such a way as to convey more of its meaning. It might be thought of as a positive or negative reaction to a word; it comes down to a personal image of the word. It is important that you explore fully your feelings about texts and try to convey as much as you can in rendering them.

There are other important considerations in interpreting a piece. Tempo is particularly important, even when metronome markings have been provided. In a "live" room, tempo must be slowed in order for nuances in inflection to be perceived. Your own ideas about the interpretation of a piece might also affect your choice of tempo. Try different tempos to see which best fits your concept of the piece.

The importance of eye contact in animating the assembly has already been discussed, but the eyes are also important in communicating the essence of a piece. Eye contact is particularly effective at the end of a thought. It punctuates what you have to say and actively involves your listeners.

The eyes and face can communicate a wide range of emotions and feelings. Dropping the eyes may indicate shame or sorrow. Raising the eyes just above the heads of the assembly, looking into the distance, may be appropriate for addressing God, even though God is present in the assembly.

Finally, memorize the piece if you can. Always keep the assembly in mind, imagining them before you as you practice. Draw on your own belief in what you are singing and recall life experiences which help you to relate to the text. Of course, there will be difficult days, days when your mood does not fit that of your assigned psalm or song, and even days when your faith has been shaken. You still have the same responsibilities on such days. You have a role to play and a duty to no less than the prayer of the church. Use memory or the power of your imagination to rejoice when you are sad, to be serious when you feel giddy, and to exhibit faith on days when faith is

---

Attending to Words

Try to speak/sing the underlined words with as much feeling/meaning as possible.

Lord, let us see your kindness, and grant us your salvation.

Lord, come and save us.

My soul rejoices in my God.

Be merciful, O Lord, for we have sinned.

Out of the depths I cry to you, O Lord.

Let my tongue be silenced if I ever forget you.

Taste and see the goodness of the Lord.

My God, why have you abandoned me?

Like a deer that longs for running streams, my soul longs for you, my God.

weak. The bottom line is this: You must believe what you are singing and you must work to make others believe. Use your face, your
eyes and your entire self to do so, but in a way that is authentic and
unaffected. Allow yourself to be personally involved in every song's
praise, prayer or lament.

Interpretation Check

Ask yourself the following questions from time to time regarding your
interpretation of cantor repertory.

Have I really done my homework or am I simply "emoting" rather than
interpreting?

Do I truly believe in what I am singing?

Practice

The need for regular and routine practice has already been stressed. Once you have established a time for practice, you will need to find a place where you can be free of distractions. It is helpful to have access to a keyboard instrument in order to locate pitches. A number of inexpensive electronic keyboards are now available, if you do not have access to a piano or organ. If you are not comfortable with a keyboard instrument, be sure to use it for pitch references only. The last thing you need is to concern yourself with learning two instruments simultaneously.

There are certain other tools which are important in a practice situation. A metronome is a very useful reference for tempos and for checking your ability to maintain a steady beat. As mentioned before, a mirror is useful for checking posture, the jaw and tongue, and body language. If you can, try to have a full-length mirror close by. A cassette recorder can help you to evaluate your own progress. If you have access to a music stand, use it. You will have greater freedom to practice gestures and a relaxed posture for singing. You may also need your hands to check for such things as a relaxed jaw.

A dictionary of musical terms and notation is essential for anyone who has not studied music and is often helpful for those who have. Many such dictionaries are available (for example, *Elson's Pocket Music Dictionary* by Louis C. Elson, published by Oliver Ditson Company).

The first thing you do in a practice session will depend upon what you have already done in a given day. Assuming that you have not yet sung, you should begin with gentle vocalization. As mentioned earlier, humming is especially good. (So is sighing aloud, whimpering and groaning.) Begin in the lower to middle portion of your range (your range is the entire compass of notes which you can comfortably sing). If you are more comfortable descending, begin with a five-note descending scale, as illustrated below. If you prefer, use an ascending scale (see below). In both cases, transpose the figure upward (or downward) by half steps.

Whenever you vocalize, remember to practice proper posture. Be certain that your face is relaxed and that your lips are loosely together for humming. You should feel a buzzing sensation at the front of your mouth and even in parts of your face. Do not attempt to hum too high in your range (past what is comfortable). Strive for a smooth, even, connected sound. Experiment with both [m] and [n]. These will produce slightly different effects for different people. If you are having trouble in achieving a forward buzzing sensation, try [n]. If your voice is generally very nasal (if you sound as if you sing and talk through your nose), use an [m].

Any variation on the five-note pattern might be your next step. Some examples have been provided below. To continue, incorporate humming with a vowel sound. Use [n] or [m] and combine it with your best vowel.

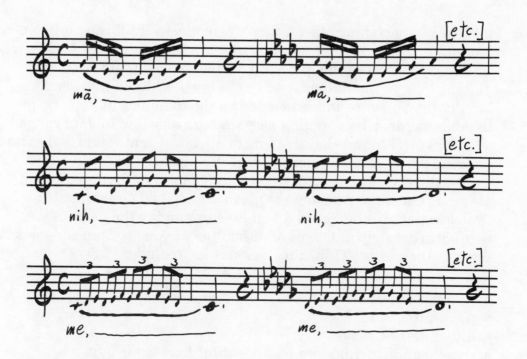

The amount of time which should be spent on gentle vocalization will vary from one person to another. As your voice becomes accustomed to singing, you should attempt to put more energy behind it. You should not force the voice, but if you do not use it to its capacity, you will never become vocally strong. For the sake of example, allow at least 15 minutes for the warm-up described thus far. This can also be your vocal warm-up prior to a liturgy or rehearsal. Of course, you can include any exercises that are helpful to you and which address a problem area in your singing, such as breathing or articulation.

The next step in your practice session involves the actual music which you are working on for your ministry. If you are going to practice several pieces, begin with the easiest and work through to the most difficult (otherwise you might abandon good vocalization for

---

Practice Session

1) Sigh, whimper, groan and hum to warm up the voice.

2) Continue with a five-note descending/ascending scale.

3) Incorporate singing and vary the pattern of the scale.

4) Move to exercises addressing your specific vocal problems.

5) Practice your music, beginning with the easiest pieces.

the sake of overcoming other difficulties of musicianship and interpretation).

Begin by singing the piece on a single vowel (your best). If the piece is long or unfamiliar, you might break it down into sections. Modify the vowel sound as needed in the extremes of your range. In other words, when singing very high or very low in your range, alter the vowel sound slightly to maintain consistent sound and ease of production. This is a normal part of singing.

Next, speak the piece in rhythm, or chant it in rhythm on a single pitch. Particular care must be given to crisp and clear articulation.

Now put together the text and tune by singing the piece as written. Try to note any problems or difficulties as you go. Stop and mark them in the music. Things to look out for include:

- running out of air
- pitch problems
- difficulties of range
- vowel sounds which are less beautiful than your best

In striving for consistency of sound, be certain to match all sounds to your best sound. It is a common error to modify a truly beautiful vowel or pitch in order to match it with the rest of the voice which may not as yet be as beautiful.

Having indicated problems in the music, you can now focus your attention on them. These problems should be removed from the context of the music and practiced slowly and carefully. The example below will give you an idea. If you continue to go over a musical passage without correcting flaws, you are actually solidifying them. Rectify problems one by one before restoring these excerpts to the context of the music.

1) Look out for the accidental. (An accidental is a flat, sharp or natural which occurs independently of the key signature.)

2) Be careful of intonation for this "leap."

3) Be careful not to go flat for descent.

4) Be careful not to run out of air.

5) Be careful to sing legato, connected.

The length of your practice will depend on the size of your task and the endurance of your voice. It will probably be necessary to rest your voice briefly during a practice session. Use these breaks to mark music and to think about body language, gestures and interpretation. When your voice becomes very tired you should stop. You may perhaps want to divide your practice into two daily sessions of shorter duration. At any rate, your practice should last from 15 minutes (post warm-up) to an hour.

Practicing a Piece

1) Divide the piece into phrases or small sections.

2) Hum and sing sections on a single vowel until comfortable.

3) Speak the text in rhythm or chant it on a single pitch.

4) Combine text and tune, still practicing small sections.

5) Isolate and concentrate on problem areas.

6) Return problem sections to the context of the piece and practice larger sections.

7) Sing through the piece in its entirety.

8) Continue to work the piece for interpretation.

Practicing a Piece with Others

1) Check for introductions, interludes, and any added time between stanzas or verses.

2) Check for balance between the voice and the instruments in the acoustical environment of the worship space.

3) Check for mutual rhythmic precision and consistency of tempo. (To rectify problems, you can remove them from the context of the music. For practice purposes, try the following: Slow the tempo; speed the tempo; clap, speak or chant the rhythm; try a staccato/very short style of execution.)

4) Check for intonation problems. Ask yourself the following with regard to problems of intonation. Do I lack support? Am I running out of air? Is there tension in my jaw or tongue? Am I maintaining proper posture? Am I sustaining energy through long notes and phrases? Do I overshoot descending/ascending lines? Am I struggling with the difficulty of the piece? Do I need to compensate for an acoustical space that is dull? Have I had adequate rest? Am I having difficulty hearing the instruments? Are the instruments out of tune?

R elated Concerns

When Is a Cantor Not a Cantor?

Much has already been said here about the cantor's craft, but we still need to ask about this ministry: What is it and what is it not? It should be clear by this point that the cantor is not merely someone who pops out from the choir. Choir members have their own distinct ministry which is related to but not the same as the ministry of the cantor. With special training and preparation a choir member could become a cantor, but not all choristers are cantor material. Similarly, the cantor is not just any vocal soloist who comes along, paid or volunteer. Certain gifts of communication and spirituality should be evident in anyone who serves as a vocal soloist in the church, but the ministry of the cantor involves an ongoing commitment to the assembly, a commitment to their sung participation and to their prayer.

The cantor is not (at the same time) the organist. If an organist is able to serve as a cantor, this is a blessing, but one does not serve as cantor from behind an organ console. It would be better to have this person stand before the assembly and sing without accompaniment. Furthermore, it is our obligation to invite many people to the variety of music ministries available, even though it sometimes seems easier for one person to do everything.

Like other ministries, the ministry of the cantor is unique. It requires special gifts and a great deal of commitment. It is a musical, liturgical and pastoral ministry which is both rooted in tradition and thoroughly modern.

The Cantor and Others

The cantor's ministry is not merely functional, and though it is distinct, it is not independent of other ministries. From time to time cantors must evaluate how they work with other ministers and within the community in general. As in any relationship, communication is essential. Ask the following questions:

How do I interact with other members of the community? Do I keep to myself, do I interact with those people I like or do I try to open myself up to interaction with the community as a whole, even to confrontation?

How do I interact with other ministers of music? Am I competitive, excessively demanding or uncharitable? Am I self-righteous? Am I supportive and affirming? Do I feel supported and affirmed? How do I deal with conflict? Am I indifferent to the ministry of others or do I feel a kinship through our common ministry?

How is musical and liturgical preparation accomplished in our community and how do I fit in? Do I make decisions by myself or in consultation with others? Does another person or persons make these decisions, and if so, how are they arrived at? Am I interested in the process, am I indifferent, or do I have strong feelings about it? What are my feelings based upon? How do I make my feelings known?

What relationship do I have to those who preside at liturgy? Have I had an opportunity to get to know the presiders? Do I feel at odds with any presider, and if so, why? How do I deal with these feelings? Do I feel supported and affirmed by presiders, and do I offer support and affirmation?

Do I think of my ministry only in terms of some portion of my life or do I live my life in the context of my ministry? Do I conduct myself in a way which is appropriate to my public ministry? Do I take ample time for prayer or am I too busy? How do I keep Sundays and the various liturgical seasons? Do I keep the seasons only in the context of Sunday liturgy, or do I keep certain days of the season (such as the Fridays of Lent), or am I conscious of the seasons as a way of guiding my life and prayer? Do I attend weekly liturgy only when I am scheduled as cantor, or do I worship with the community on a weekly basis throughout the year? Is Jesus at the core of my life and ministry?

How do I take care of myself? Is all of my free time spent in the service of the church? Am I using my ministry to avoid family commitments and relationships? Am I unable to say "no" to any request for service? Am I heading for ministerial burnout? What are my true motives for ministry?

Beyond Sunday Morning

It is also good to examine the ways the various sacraments and rites of the church are celebrated in your parish and what role the cantor plays. Too often weddings, funerals and baptisms are not treated as communal celebrations of the parish, but as private events. As such, vocal soloists are used more often than cantors, if there is music at all. The assembly is rarely invited to sing. Cantors are most needed in situations where people are least likely to sing of their own accord. Communal singing can and should be a part of these celebrations.

A cantor should take time prior to the beginning of these liturgies to introduce congregational materials and to elicit initial responses from the assembly. Congregational materials should be simple and well known. It is not necessary that everything be sung, but certainly the responsorial psalm and gospel acclamation should be sung as a part of any liturgy of the word. For eucharistic liturgies, the "Holy, holy," the memorial acclamation and the great Amen should be sung. Beyond this, choose from appropriate songs, hymns and psalms which are commonly known or easy to enter into.

Preparation with Other
Liturgical Ministers

For all celebrations, large and small, the cantor must be prepared. But this does not apply to the cantor alone. Preparation and even rehearsal should happen with all liturgical ministers involved in a celebration. Some of this preparation is individual, but there are points at which ministries interact or merge.

Those involved in a celebration as cantor, lector, presider, acolyte, deacon, eucharistic minister and any others should come together to discuss and even to walk through the specific celebration. The Sunday liturgy during Ordinary Time should be carefully learned by all ministers as individuals and as ensemble. Variations in this order for Advent, Christmastime, Lent and Eastertime will need reminders and rehearsals each year. Walking through the liturgy is especially important in the case of once-a-year liturgies, such as those of the Triduum. If ministers are unwilling to come together for this purpose, they have no business coming together to celebrate liturgy. In the liturgy each of us is not invited to do his or her own thing. We do the Christian community's thing. Instruction sheets and memos are useful, but successful liturgy does not simply spring from the head. It must be in the very bones of those who bear its awesome responsibility.

The cantor cannot determine how other ministers will conduct themselves, but can model a way of doing ministry. Neither success nor failure is in your hands. Simply allow yourself to be God's tool.

Inclusive Language

The texts which a cantor sings may present special problems. Many people have become sensitive to the preponderance of masculine language and imagery found in the liturgy of the church. While traditional hymns have been reworked and new songs have been written with this sensitivity in mind, the designated texts of the liturgy are not as easily changed. The church continues to struggle with new translations of the psalter, of various prayers and of all of scripture, but the process is lengthy. It involves the consultation and collaboration of biblical scholars, poets, theologians, liturgists and liturgical musicians.

The sung texts of the liturgy should not be changed casually or arbitrarily by anyone who feels inclined to do so. The poetry of the language can easily be lost. Even the changing of hymns and song texts must be handled carefully and on an individual basis.

There are times when language can and should be changed. Such changes should be carefully thought out in consultation with others. Pastoral concern, and not politicizing the liturgy, should determine the changes. Pastoral considerations must be inclusive of the entire community. Alongside the need for language which expresses the equality of all people in the eyes of God, consider the need in ritual for familiarity and consistency.

The pastoral judgment does not stand alone. It must be considered with musical and liturgical appropriateness. The musical judgment would require an appropriate wedding of text and music. The liturgical judgment would raise questions of symbolic and theological integrity. All three judgments require intelligibility of text. An approach which considers the liturgy in this way will lead to positive and long-lasting changes in the language of worship. Hasty changes will only create further problems and may delay the transformation of our communal prayer.

Appendix: An Evening of Recollection

Who ministers to the ministers? This question frequently emerges when ministers gather for a few moments of soul-searching. Who comes to mop their feverish brows in the heat of ministering? Who cares that they care? Church musicians wonder about this as they continue to minister with singing and playing Sunday after Sunday. One could almost see in them a replica of a religious community bound to celebrate the liturgy, called to leave family and friends to do just that and do it as if it were a lifetime commitment. For most in the music ministry of the church, the term of service is for life. The weekly rehearsal and the weekly celebration are as certain as Sunday itself. As the sign says, "We never close."

When those ministers show signs of tuckering out by their hatefulness, boredom and cantankerous behavior, then some type of oasis is not only desirable—it is necessary. Gallons of wine and wheels of cheese are helpful pacifiers, but there is a spiritual renewal that is necessary also. These ministers need to be ministered unto. They need to be nourished with God's word and God's presence in each other. Such revelations are a little hampered on a Sunday morning while music is shuffled and instruments go out of tune. Music ministers need to draw aside in prayerful reflection with the language that is their own. That language is the music with which they minister. The difference is that during this time, the music should be permitted to enlighten and comfort them. The music should anoint as well as express.

The scheme suggested here incorporates two principles. The first is that the music used be familiar and cherished by the musicians. These musical items are chosen for the charm they have wielded on the ministers. The charm has the power to speak anew by the force of the more relaxed format in which it is being performed. The music now has the chance to touch the heart of the performer. It can minister.

The second principle is that the ministers need to be cared for and not asked to do the caring. They do that every time they celebrate the liturgy. In this format there is no time assigned to small group discussions or story sharing. In fact, the contrary is true. Much time is allowed for listening and responding with music. They shall sing in the course of the exercise, but the song is for each singer. And God is praised in all of that.

The time assigned for such an exercise or period of recollection is the same as the regular weekly rehearsal session, a clear indication that this is important enough to suspend the sacrosanct rehearsal. Clever planning absorbs and adjusts such a relinquishing of rehearsal time. For many music ministers, that weekly rehearsal carries the weight of a holy day of obligation worthy enough to disrupt domestic and social schedules. The leader of the session should be the leader of the ministries, the parish's minister of music and liturgy. In more places than ever before, this music minister provides a spiritual leadership most unique in the music groups. He or she discovers that valid liturgical leadership is more than just leading the ensemble and assembly in hymns, psalms and spiritual canticles. There is a genuine interconnectedness between musical direction and prayer direction. "Let us sing" is actually "Let us pray." Here is an opportunity for a cultivation of that leadership.

After a period of "direct interpersonal encountership"—that is to say, eating and drinking and gossiping—the group is called together by the leader and led in three sung items. The mood changes with each item. From a "kicker" type item to a more introspective one, the music has a chance to effect some of its power. For example:

"Praise him! Praise him!" *Worship II*, 227
"Come down, O Love divine" (Down Ampney)
"O Lord, hear my prayer" Berthier (Taizé)

These items should be compiled in one leaflet to avoid shuffling and searching. The leader prefaces this first experience with an invitation to their prayer, calling to mind their ministry and reason for gathering. Such remarks are concluded with an invitation to silence. The silence is interrupted with the introduction of the first hymn.

After the last item has settled into everyone's musical psyche, the leader prays one of the "Venite" psalms (95, 96, 97, 98, 99 or 100). Silence follows.

Two items are suggested here to interrupt this silence. The Byzantine setting of the Beatitudes joined by Peloquin's "Lord Jesus, you are here with us" is a powerful sequence of musical experiences. Both items require great discipline and should be an established part of the group's repertory. Another set would be Marty Haugen's "Shepherd me, O God" and "There is a balm in Gilead." The mood is one of comfort and tranquility, two elements frequently missing on Sunday morning.

In the silence which follows, all listen to a piece of religious repertory (e.g., depending on the season, excerpts from Handel's *Messiah* with texts—not scores—can provide a strong scriptural commentary on that season). Here is some space to listen to what the choir might have sung that past year.

After this listening part, the director could offer some story or reflection that provides witness to his or her ministry with the group or other groups. In all of the telling, the reflection should be strongly affirmative.

After a shorter period of silence, a lengthy selection of scripture would be read. Psalm 34—read with great care and deliberation and with large pauses—is a powerful psalm of confidence and healing. This reading can be followed with two settings of the same psalm: "O taste and see" by Ralph Vaughan Williams and "Taste and see" by James Moore.

At this point some music ministers will be frustrated to desperation that the group has yet to break into small groups to discuss what they were talking about in the refreshment period at the beginning of the event. So, if you wish, this would be the time for the group to disperse and do private reading of scripture, of the psalms, or of the text of one of the musical items so designated by the director. After 20 minutes, the group reconvenes.

Two Taizé items call the group back into reflection: "Jesus, remember me" and "Laudate Dominum." The leader reflects briefly upon the ministry they share, a ministry to serve the liturgical assembly and its praise of God. This reflection segues into some form of intercession. The Byzantine formula is consistently successful. Shared prayer and petitions follow, concluding with the singing of the Lord's Prayer. The leader imparts the Aaronic blessing and an invitation to sing something like David Hurd's "Christ, mighty savior" which provides a gracious and moving completion to this evening of prayer.

—*Fred Moleck*

Music Acknowledgments

The English translation of the psalm responses and Lenten gospel acclamations from the *Lectionary for Mass* © 1969, International Committee on English in the Liturgy, Inc. (ICEL); excerpts from the English translation of the *Rite of Funerals* © 1970, ICEL; the English translation of the Canticle of the Lamb from *The Liturgy of the Hours* © 1974, ICEL; music from *Music for the Rite of Funerals and Rite of Baptism for Children* © 1977, music for the Canticle of the Lamb from the *Resource Collection of Hymns and Service Music for the Liturgy* © 1977, ICEL; music by Willcock and Mews for psalm refrains from *ICEL Lectionary Music: Psalms and Alleluia and Gospel Acclamations for the Liturgy of the Word* © 1982, ICEL. All rights reserved.

Page 7. "In the silent hours." Psalm 134. Text: ICEL. Music: Howard Hughes, SM. Copyright © 1986 by GIA Publications, Inc., Chicago IL. All rights reserved.

Page 8. "Alleluia, alleluia." Canticle of the Lamb, Revelation 19:1-7. Music: Howard Hughes, SM. Copyright ICEL.

Page 9. "Jesus is the image." Colossians 1:12-20. Music: Robert LeBlanc. Copyright © 1986 by GIA Publications, Inc., Chicago IL. All rights reserved.

Page 10. "I will praise." Refrain: copyright ICEL. Psalm 63: New American Bible, copyright © 1969, 1970 by the Confraternity of the Christian Doctrine. Music for psalm: copyright © 1984, Richard Proulx.